How Many Are Here?

By Meish Goldish

Illustrated by
Jill Meyerhoff

Sadlier-Oxford
A Division of William H. Sadlier, Inc.

How many plates are here?
Count how many.

How many cups are here?
Count how many.

How many hamburgers are here?
Count how many.

4

How many hot dogs are here?
Count how many.

How many apples are here?
Count how many.

How many strawberries are here?
Count how many.

How many ants are here?
Too many!